COOKIES
for SANTA

LAUGHING ELEPHANT BOOKS • MMIX

LAUGHING ELEPHANT BOOKS

Copyright © 2009 Blue Lantern Studio • All Rights Reserved • Second Printing

ISBN 978-1-59583-375-4

3645 Interlake Avenue North • Seattle • Washington • 98103 • www.LAUGHINGELELPHANT.com

Printed in China

TABLE OF CONTENTS

LEAVING COOKIES FOR SANTA

Santa Claus loves cookies - cookies of all kinds: bar cookies, drop cookies, roll cookies and fridge cookies. Frankly, Kris Kringle is a little indiscriminate in his cookie consumption, so when leaving cookies for Santa, don't worry, he is easy to please. That being said, there are a few tips to ensure that Santa is especially pleased with your cookie offering and perhaps will leave an extra gift or two under your tree.

First of all, Santa prefers home-made cookies, which isn't to say that he is a snob (perish the thought! Santa enjoys Nutter Butters, Oreos and Thin Mints along with the rest of the populace) but rather that he likes to know that we made an extra-special effort for him on this his extra-special day.

Secondly, Santa likes milk with his cookies. This is very important as he can become quite un-jolly if, after eating a few tasty, but rather dry, chocolate crispies, there is nothing to wash them down with. A tall, plain glass of milk is preferred (whole milk if available); room temperature is fine. Warm cocoa or a little pot of tea (your choice) can be a nice touch but by no means necessary; Santa loves a good glass of milk.

Third on the list of advice for leaving cookies for Saint Nick is the delicate subject of how many cookies to leave. If you ask Mrs. Claus you will get an entirely different answer than that of her husband. She would answer, "Do you have to leave any at all? I am trying to keep him on his diet; couldn't you leave a nice rice cake instead?" And he would simply say, "How many can you spare?" In the end you, the cookie leaver, have to decide. We recommend that you take a fair amount of cookies for yourself and your family, as Santa loves to share even more than he loves cookies, and leave the remainder that will fit in a single layer on your plate of choice.

The location of the milk and cookies is next on our list and it is not a trifle we have blithely thrown in to fill pages. Santa is very busy on Christmas Eve, and if he has to hunt around for your offerings not only is the gesture's joy diminished but also you may have slowed Father Christmas on his appointed rounds. Therefore, place the cookies in plain, visual sight of the Christmas tree. That's all; Santa will do the rest.

Finally, do not attempt to hide and catch a glimpse of Santa; contrary to some popular myths, he does not appreciate this. If Santa needs to, he will contact and make himself known to you. He is a busy man; let him do his job.

A FEW FINAL THOUGHTS;

• Santa enjoys a nice note; a short 'Merry Christmas' or 'We Love You, Santa!' is sufficient.

• Yes, do leave a carrot or two for the reindeer, no sugar cubes please.

• A decorated Christmas-y cookie plate and festive Holiday napkin are nice touches but by no means required.

• Have fun, Santa does.

NOTES ON THE RECIPES IN THIS BOOK:

The recipes in this book are drawn from an extensive collection of vintage cooking pamphlets, circa 1900 - 1960. As such, the sponsoring companies put them together with great care, as the recipe carried the brand name of the product, and thus the reputation of the company, along with it. Therefore, the cook can be assured that these recipes have been extensively tested but should keep in mind that, particularly among the older recipes, preferences and cooking customs may have changed, and adjust accordingly or, as we recommend, enjoy a little culinary anthropology.

Alice Cookies

INGREDIENTS

½ cup butter or margarine

1 cup broken nut pieces

¾ cup sugar

1 teaspoon baking powder

2 eggs

1 cup flour

½ teaspoon salt

¼ cup milk

1 teaspoon cinnamon

½ cup coconut

1 cup oatmeal

DIRECTIONS

Preheat oven to 350°

Blend shortening and sugar, add eggs and milk, then coconut, raisins and nuts. Sift salt, baking powder and cinnamon with flour, and add to oatmeal. Add to first mixture and stir thoroughly. Drop from spoon onto greased pan.

Bake for 12 minutes.

Makes about 50 cookies.

from *The Delineator Magazine,* 1929

INGREDIENTS

1 cup butter or margarine

1 cup brown sugar

2 eggs well beaten

1 cup molasses

2 teaspoons cinnamon

½ teaspoon baking soda

1 cup hot coffee

1 teaspoon vinegar

4 cups flour

2 teaspoons ginger

3 teaspoons baking powder

1 teaspoon salt

DIRECTIONS

Preheat oven to 350°

Blend sugar and shortening, add well beaten egg, molasses, spices and baking soda which had been mixed into the hot coffee. Then add vinegar and beat in the flour that has been previously sifted with salt and baking powder. Stir well and drop from end of spoon onto greased cookie sheets.

Bake for 10 minutes.

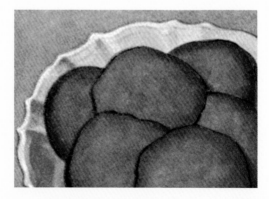

from *The Delineator Magazine,* 1929

INGREDIENTS

½ cup peanut butter

¼ cup butter or margarine

½ cup brown sugar

½ cup granulated sugar

1 egg, well beaten

1 cup sifted all-purpose flour

1 teaspoon baking soda

DIRECTIONS

Preheat oven to 350°

Cream peanut butter and shortening together. Add sugar gradually, continuing to cream until mixture is light and fluffy. Add beaten egg. Sift flour and baking soda together, add; mix well. Drop mixture, one level teaspoon at a time, on cookie sheet. Press down with tines of a fork; press a second time so that creases are at right angles. Bake 10-15 minutes. Makes about 4 dozen cookies.

from a cookie sheet label, circa 1950

INGREDIENTS

½ cup butter or margarine

½ cup granulated sugar

¼ cup firmly packed brown sugar

1 egg

1 teaspoon vanilla

1 cup flour

½ teaspoon baking soda

½ teaspoon salt

1 cup (6 ounces) chocolate chips

½ cup chopped nuts

DIRECTIONS

Preheat oven to 375°

Beat shortening, sugars, egg, and vanilla until light and fluffy. Blend in flour, baking soda, and salt; stir in chips and nuts. Drop by teaspoonfuls, 2 inches apart, onto un-greased baking sheets. Bake 8 to 10 minutes, or until lightly browned. Makes about 4 dozen cookies.

from *Baker's Chocolate & Coconut Favorites*, 1952

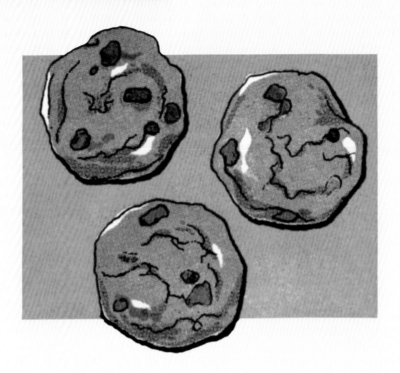

INGREDIENTS

1 cup butter or margarine

2 cups brown sugar (packed)

2 eggs

½ cup sour milk or buttermilk (or milk to which 1½ teaspoons of vinegar has been added)

3½ cups flour

½ teaspoon baking soda

1 teaspoon salt

3 to 4 cups cut-up gum drops

DIRECTIONS

Preheat oven to 400°

Mix shortening, brown sugar, eggs. Stir in sour milk. Sift dry ingredients together and stir in. Mix in gumdrops. Chill at least one hour. Drop rounded teaspoonfuls about 2″ apart on a lightly greased baking sheet. Bake about 8 to 10 minutes, or until set.

Makes about 6 dozen 2½″ cookies.

from *Candy Cookies*, circa 1950

INGREDIENTS

1½ cups flour

½ teaspoon salt

1 cup sugar

3 ounces unsweetened chocolate, melted

¾ cup seedless raisins

EASY FROSTING:

2 cups sifted confectioner's sugar

1 teaspoon vanilla

1½ teaspoons baking powder

½ cup butter or margarine

2 eggs slightly beaten

1 teaspoon vanilla

½ cup milk

2 tablespoons hot milk

DIRECTIONS

Preheat oven to 350°

Sift together flour, baking powder and salt; set aside. Cream shortening thoroughly; gradually beat in sugar and beat until well blended. Add eggs and chocolate; beat well. Stir in vanilla and raisins. Add dry ingredients alternately with the milk, a little at a time and blend well. Cover and chill about one hour. Drop dough by rounded teaspoonfuls onto cookie sheets about 2″ apart. Bake 12-15 minutes. Remove from pans; cool on wire racks. When cold, spread with frosting and decorate.

Makes about 5 dozen.

EASY FROSTING:

Stir hot milk into confectioner's sugar, add vanilla. Mix to smooth consistency. Divide into three parts and color with food coloring.

from *Foodarama Party Book*, 1959

Ginger Cookies

INGREDIENTS

5 cups sifted flour

4 teaspoons baking powder

1½ teaspoons salt

1½ teaspoons baking soda

1 tablespoon cinnamon

1 cup butter

1½ cups firmly packed brown sugar

3 eggs, well beaten

1 tablespoon ginger

½ cup dark molasses

1½ cups boiling water

1 cup finely chopped walnuts or peanuts

DIRECTIONS

Preheat oven to 400°

Mix and sift the flour, baking powder, salt, baking soda, and cinnamon and set aside. In a mixing bowl, beat the butter until creamy. Add the sugar gradually and continue beating until light. Stir in eggs and beat well. Combine ginger and molasses, add to the sugar mixture and stir well. Gradually add the boiling water, stirring constantly. Add flour mixture gradually and stir to mix well. Cover the bowl and chill 2 hours or longer.

Drop dough by rounded teaspoonfuls, about 2 inches apart, onto greased baking sheets and sprinkle with chopped nuts.

Bake 10 to 12 minutes. Remove from pans and cool on cake racks.

Makes about 7 dozen.

from *Cooky Jar Favorites*, 1956

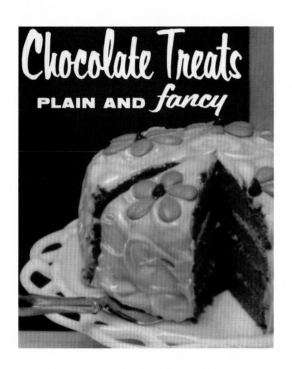

INGREDIENTS

2 squares (1 ounce each) unsweetened chocolate.

Dash of salt

½ teaspoon vanilla

1 can (14 ounces) sweetened condensed milk

1 cup coarsely chopped pecans

DIRECTIONS

Preheat oven to 350°

Melt unsweetened chocolate. Add salt, vanilla and sweetened condensed milk; stir until well blended. Add and stir in coarsely chopped pecans. Drop by teaspoonfuls about 3 inches apart on a greased cookie sheet.

Bake 10 to 12 minutes. Let stand about 1 minute on sheet. Remove wafers with a lightly greased spatula to a wire rack; cool.

Makes about 36 wafers.

from *Chocolate Treats Plain and Fancy,* 1953

Applesauce Cookies

INGREDIENTS

½ cup butter or margarine

1 cup sugar

1 egg

1 cup applesauce

2½ cups sifted enriched flour

1 teaspoon baking powder

½ teaspoon salt

½ teaspoon baking soda

¼ teaspoon ground cloves

½ teaspoon cinnamon

½ cup seedless raisins

½ cup chopped nuts

DIRECTIONS

Preheat oven to 375°

Blend shortening, sugar and egg and add applesauce. Stir in combined dry ingredients, then raisins and nuts. Drop from teaspoon 2″ apart on a greased baking sheet.

Bake about 10 minutes or until lightly browned.

Makes about 7 dozen cookies.

from *Praise for the Cook*, 1959

INGREDIENTS

½ cup butter or margarine

½ cup sugar

1 tablespoon instant coffee

1 egg

¾ cup sifted enriched flour

½ teaspoon baking powder

½ teaspoon salt

½ teaspoon vanilla

½ cup chopped nuts

DIRECTIONS

Preheat oven to 375°

Blend shortening, sugar and coffee. Add egg. Stir in combined dry ingredients. Beat vigorously until batter is smooth. Fold in vanilla and nuts. Drop from a teaspoon 2½" apart on an un-greased baking sheet.

Bake about 12 minutes or until lightly browned.

Makes about 2½ dozen cookies.

from *Praise for the Cook*, 1959

INGREDIENTS

½ cup butter

1½ cups sugar

1½ teaspoons vanilla

½ teaspoon almond extract

2 large eggs, well beaten

2¾ cups sifted flour

1 teaspoon salt

½ teaspoon baking powder

½ teaspoon baking soda

1 cup sour cream

1½ cups seedless raisins

½ cup candied cherries or mixed candied fruits, chopped

butter frosting

DIRECTIONS

Preheat oven to 375°

Beat shortening, sugar and flavorings until fluffy. Beat in eggs. Sift flour, salt, baking powder and baking soda together. Add to sugar alternately with sour cream. Stir in fruits and raisins. Drop dough in small mounds 2 inches apart onto greased baking sheets.

Bake 8 to 10 minutes. Cool cookies. Ice with butter frosting. Decorate with raisins and candied fruits.

Makes about 3½ dozen.

BUTTER FROSTING:

Cream ½ cup (I stick) butter until light and fluffy. Add ⅛ teaspoon salt, 1 teaspoon vanilla and 2 cups confectioners' sugar, beating until smooth. Beat in cream, 1 tablespoon at a time, until desired consistency is reached.

from *Delicious New Raisin Recipes*, 1964

INGREDIENTS

2 ½ cups sifted flour

1 teaspoon baking soda

⅔ cup butter or margarine

1½ cups sugar

2 eggs

2 tablespoons molasses

½ tablespoon salt

1 tablespoon cinnamon

½ cup 7-Up

2 cups rolled oats

1 cup chopped nuts

1 cup raisins

DIRECTIONS

Preheat oven to 450°

Sift flour with baking soda. Mix shortening, sugar and eggs until creamy. Blend in molasses, salt and cinnamon. Mix in 7-Up alternately with flour mixture. Blend in oats, nuts, and raisins. Drop dough by teaspoonfuls, 2″ apart, onto lightly greased cookie sheet.

Bake for 8 to 10 minutes. Remove from baking sheet and cool on wire rack.

Makes about 80 cookies.

from *Put the Un in Cooking Fun with 7-Up*, 1969

INGREDIENTS

½ cup (¼ lb.) softened butter

½ cup sugar

1 egg yolk

¼ cup sour cream

1 teaspoon vanilla

1 cup sifted flour

¼ cup chopped maraschino cherries

¼ cup coarsely chopped nuts

DIRECTIONS

Preheat oven to 375°

Cream butter, sugar, egg yolk and sour cream until smooth. Stir in vanilla. Add flour; blend well. Stir in cherries and nuts. Drop by tea-spoonfuls on cookie sheet.

Bake 10 to 12 minutes, or until brown. Cool on wire racks.

Makes about 3 dozen.

from *Tips for Teens*, 1967

Picture from
Osterizer Recipes, 1964

Picture from *Cooking with a
Surprise Difference,* 1966

What's a rainy day for?

Picture from *Mary Alden's Cake and Cookie Cookbook for Children*, 1956

INGREDIENTS

1 cup soft butter or margarine

1 cup sugar

2 eggs

1 cup (about 2) mashed bananas

½ cup undiluted evaporated milk

1 tablespoon vinegar

1 teaspoon vanilla

3 cups sifted flour

1½ teaspoons baking soda

1½ teaspoon salt

1 cup chopped walnuts

DIRECTIONS

Preheat oven to 375°

Blend butter, sugar, eggs, banana, evaporated milk, vinegar and vanilla until light and fluffy. Sift flour, baking soda and salt together. Blend into banana mixture. Stir in walnuts. Chill 1 hour. Drop rounded spoonfuls 2 inches apart on lightly buttered cookie sheet.

Bake about 15 minutes. Cool and top with Vanilla Icing, if desired.

VANILLA ICING:

Combine 2½ cups sifted confectioners' sugar with 2 tablespoons soft butter, ¼ cup undiluted evaporated milk and ¼ teaspoon vanilla. Beat until smooth. Spread over jumbos and top with walnuts.

from *Cooking with A Surprising Difference*, 1966

from *All About Home Baking,* 1933

Picture from *Coconut, Sun-sweetness from the Tropics*, 1928

INGREDIENTS

2 cups flour

2 teaspoons baking powder

1 tablespoon grated orange rind

4 tablespoons butter or margarine

1 cup sugar

1 egg, unbeaten

¼ cup milk

½ cup orange juice

4 tablespoons sugar

1 egg white, stiffly beaten

3 ounces shredded coconut

DIRECTIONS

Preheat oven to 350°

Sift flour once, measure, add baking powder, and sift together three times. Add orange rind to butter and cream thoroughly. Add sugar gradually and cream together well. Add egg and beat until light and fluffy. Add flour, alternately with milk and orange juice, a small amount at a time. Beat after each addition until smooth. Pour into a greased pan, 15 x 10 inches. Cover with a thin layer of meringue made by beating sugar into egg white. Sprinkle with coconut. Bake in moderate oven for 25 minutes. Cool. Cut into strips. Makes 2 dozen tea strips. These tea cakes are also attractive when cut into diamond shaped pieces.

Recipe from *All About Home Baking,*1933

from *All About Home Baking,*1933

Rainy Day Date Sticks

INGREDIENTS

¾ cup butter or margarine

1½ cups sugar

1 egg

1 cup buttermilk

½ teaspoon baking soda

3 cups flour

1 teaspoon salt

1 teaspoon baking powder

1 cup chopped nuts

1 cup cut dates

Powdered sugar

DIRECTIONS

Preheat oven to 350°

Blend shortening with sugar and egg briskly. Dissolve soda in buttermilk. Combine the two mixtures. Then add flour that has been sifted with salt and baking powder. Fold in nuts and dates. Pour into two shallow pans or one large cookie sheet, greased.

Bake 20 – 25 minutes. Cut into narrow slices when still warm and roll in powdered sugar

DIRECTIONS

Preheat oven to 400°

To melted chocolate add butter, sugar, eggs, flour, and vanilla, beating well. Spread mixture on a baking sheet. Sprinkle with nuts.

Bake 15 minutes. While warm cut with a cookie cutter, or mark into 2 inch squares, cool and break into squares.

Makes about 48.

INGREDIENTS

2 squares Unsweetened Chocolate, melted

½ cup butter

1 cup sugar

2 eggs

½ cup sifted flour

½ teaspoon vanilla

½ cup chopped nuts

from *Baker's Best Chocolate Recipes*, 1932

INGREDIENTS

¾ cup sifted flour

½ teaspoon baking powder

½ teaspoon salt

½ cup chopped Brazil nuts

1 cup sliced dates

2 eggs

1 cup brown sugar

DIRECTIONS

Preheat oven to 350°

Sift together the flour, baking powder and salt. Mix the Brazil nuts and dates throughout the flour. Beat eggs until light; beat in the sugar gradually. Stir into the dry ingredients, nuts and dates. Spread the mixture evenly over a well-greased shallow pan.

Bake for 30 minutes or until the surface will spring back when pressed lightly. Cut into strips 4 inches long by 1 inch wide.

With the Compliments of

KERNEL NUT OF BRAZIL

from *A Parade of Brazil Nut Recipes*, circa 1940

INGREDIENTS

Preheat oven to 350°

For bottom mixture:

Mix together:

1 cup sifted flour

2 tablespoons brown sugar

¼ teaspoon salt

Cut in:

½ cup butter or margarine to make fine crumbs.

Pat into greased pan (6"x10").

Bake 15 minutes at 350°

For top mixture:

Sift together and set aside:

¼ cup sifted flour

½ teaspoon baking powder

⅛ teaspoon salt

Beat 2 eggs until lemon-colored

Add 1½ cups brown sugar gradually, beating until thick

Stir in flour mixture, ½ teaspoon vanilla, ¾ cup shredded coconut, 8 oz package of semi-sweet chocolate chips.

Spread top mixture over baked crumb mixture.

DIRECTIONS

Preheat oven to 350°

Bake at 45 minutes

Cool slightly before removing from pan. When well cooled, cut into bars

Makes 24 bars.

from *Collectors' Items* (Nestle pamphlet)

Illustration by Eugene Iverd,
magazine cover. 1935

DIRECTIONS

Preheat oven to 350°

Beat eggs well. Beat sugar in gradually. Add butter. Combine and add nuts and fruits. Sift together flour, salt and baking powder. Combine dry ingredients with the first mixture and combine very thoroughly. Turn into a well greased 8 inch square pan.

Bake about 45 minutes. Cut into squares when cold.

INGREDIENTS

2 eggs

1 cup fruit sugar

3 tablespoons melted butter

1 cup chopped stoned dates

¾ cup chopped blanched almonds

¼ cup chopped candied cherries

¼ cup chopped candied pineapple

3 to 4½ tablespoons chopped candied ginger

¾ cup pastry flour

1 teaspoon baking powder

⅔ teaspoon salt

from *Christmas Recipes*, circa 1935

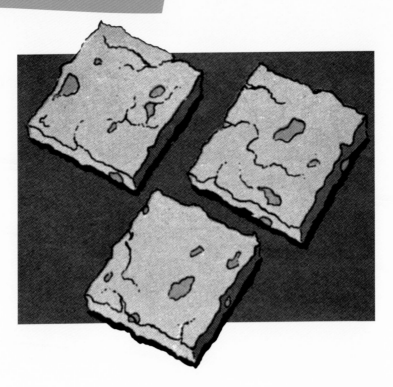

INGREDIENTS

1½ cups brown sugar (packed)

2 eggs

1⅓ cups flour

⅔ cup cut-up fresh orange slices, with white skin left on (1 large or 2 small oranges)

⅔ cup cut-up pecans

DIRECTIONS

Preheat oven to 350°

Beat sugar and eggs 3 minutes at high speed on mixer. Stir in flour. Fold in orange pieces and pecans. Spread thinly in greased jellyroll pan, 15½″ x 10½″ x 1″.

Bake 30 to 35 minutes. While warm spread thinly with glaze: mix grated rind of 1 orange, ⅔ cup sifted confectioners' sugar, 2 tablespoons cream. Cool in pan. When cool cut in 2″ x 1½″ bars.

Makes about 50 bars.

from *Candy Cookies*, circa 1950

DIRECTIONS

Preheat oven to 350°

Grease an oblong pan, 13 x 9 1/2 x 2." Blend butter, ½ cup brown sugar, granulated sugar, egg yolks and vanilla. Beat 2 minutes at medium speed on mixer, or 200 strokes by hand, scraping bowl constantly. Sift in dry ingredients and stir into creamed mixture until thoroughly mixed. Spread or pat dough into pan. Sprinkle with chocolate pieces, coconut and nuts. Beat egg whites until frothy; add 1 cup brown sugar and beat until stiff, but not dry. Spread on top of chocolate-coconut-nut mixture.

Bake 35-40 minutes. Cool and cut into bars.

Makes 40-60 bars.

INGREDIENTS

¾ cup soft butter

½ cup brown sugar (packed)

½ cup granulated sugar

3 eggs separated

1 teaspoon vanilla

2 cups flour

1 teaspoon baking powder

¼ teaspoon baking soda

¼ teaspoon salt

6 ounces chocolate pieces

1 cup flaked or grated coconut

¾ cup coarsely chopped nuts

1 cup brown sugar (packed)

from *Candy Cookies*, circa 1950

Rainbow Cookies

INGREDIENTS

2 cups sugar

1¾ cups butter

3 eggs

4½ cups flour

1 teaspoon baking powder

1 teaspoon salt

2 cups flour

1½ teaspoons orange extract

1 ounce chocolate

Food coloring

Nuts

Candy

Candied fruit or candy

DIRECTIONS

Preheat oven to 400°

Sift together 2½ cups flour, baking powder and salt. Cream shortening, and add sugar gradually, creaming thoroughly; add the eggs and orange extract, beat well. Divide into four parts, each in a different bowl, then add ½ cup flour to each bowl. Mix into one bowl the melted chocolate, into the second add red coloring to make pink dough, into the third add green coloring and leave the fourth plain. Mix all well. Again divide the dough into several small batches, placing each one on a piece of waxed paper. Combine different doughs as illustrated to make fancy cookies. Kneading into the dough nuts, dried fruits, candies etc.

Put in the refrigerator until hard, slice and bake until lightly brown.

from *Good Luck Color Scheme Parties*, 1931

DIRECTIONS

Preheat oven to 425°

Sift together flour, baking powder and salt. Cream shortening, and add both sugars gradually, creaming thoroughly; add the egg, walnut kernels, and vanilla, beat well. Add flour gradually, mixing well after each addition. Shape into rolls about 1½″ in diameter; roll in waxed paper.

Chill in refrigerator 2 hours to overnight. Cut roll into ⅛″ slices and bake on ungreased baking sheets 5-8 minutes.

INGREDIENTS

2 cups sifted flour

2 teaspoons baking powder

⅛ teaspoon salt

½ cup butter or margarine

1 cup sugar

¼ cup brown sugar, firmly packed

1 egg well beaten

1 cup chopped walnuts

1½ teaspoons vanilla extract

Picture from Magazine Illustration, 1929

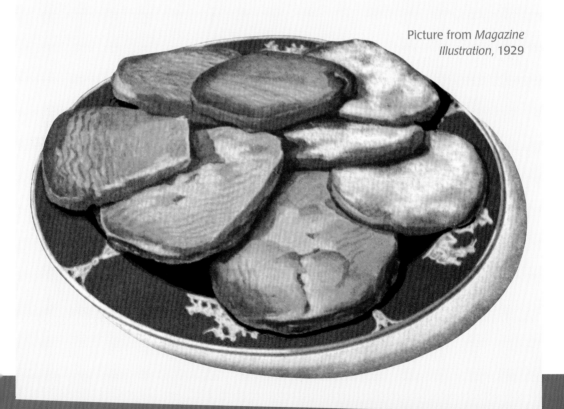

from *Menu Magic in a Nutshell*, circa 1930

from Baker's *Famous Chocolate Recipes*, 1936

Picture from
Sweet Recipes, 1950

INGREDIENTS

½ cup butter

¾ cup sugar

1 egg

1 tablespoon milk

1 teaspoon peppermint extract

1¼ cups sifted flour

¼ teaspoon salt

¼ teaspoon baking powder

1 ounce unsweetened chocolate, melted

DIRECTIONS

Preheat oven to 375°

Blend butter, sugar, egg, milk and peppermint extract. Add combined dry ingredients and mix thoroughly. Divide dough into two parts. To one half, add the chocolate and mix thoroughly. Roll each portion of dough ½″ thick on waxed paper. Dough will be soft. Place white dough on chocolate dough. Remove paper and roll. Wrap in waxed paper.

Chill 2-3 hours. Slice ¼″ thick and place on greased baking sheet. Bake about 10 minutes or until lightly browned.

Makes about 3 dozen.

from *Praise for the Cook,* 1959

Peppermint Pinwheels

Preheat oven to 375°

Mix shortening, sugar, egg, and flavorings. Mix flour and salt; blend in thoroughly. Divide dough in half. Blend red food coloring into one half. Chill doughs until firm. On a lightly floured cloth-covered board roll light half into a 12" square. Roll red half same size and lay on top of light dough. Roll double layer of dough gently until ³⁄₁₆" thick. Roll up tightly as for jellyroll.

Chill 1 hour. Slice ⅛" thick. Place on an ungreased baking sheet and bake 9 minutes, or until lightly browned. While still warm, brush with egg white glaze (recipe below) and sprinkle with mixture of candy and sugar.

Makes 6 to 7 dozen.

EGG WHITE GLAZE:

Mix 1 egg white and 2 tablespoons water.

INGREDIENTS

1 cup butter or margarine

1 cup sifted confectioners' sugar

1 egg

1½ teaspoons almond flavoring

1 teaspoon vanilla

2½ cups flour

1 teaspoon salt

½ teaspoon red food coloring

¼ cup each finely crushed peppermint stick candy and sugar, if desired.

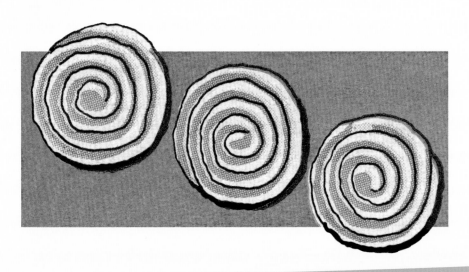

from *Candy Cookies*, circa 1950

DIRECTIONS

Preheat oven to 375°

Mix butter, sugar, salt, food coloring and lemon rind thoroughly. Add flour and blend. Roll dough into a 2" diameter log, cut in half, wrap in waxed paper & chill. Cut into ¼" slices. Sprinkle with decorator's sugar.

Bake on ungreased baking sheet, 6 to 8 minutes, until set but not brown. Cool. For effect of outside rind, roll rounded edge in mixture of 1 egg white and 1 teaspoon water then in colored sugar. Add thin line of icing (recipe below) ¼" from outside edge.

Makes about 6 dozen.

ICING:
Blend 1 cup sifted confectioners' sugar, ¼ teaspoon salt and 1 tablespoon lemon juice. Pile in pastry tube and squeeze onto cookies.

ORANGE:
Follow directions above – except mix 5 drops red liquid food coloring and 12 drops yellow liquid food coloring for orange colored cookie dough. (Food coloring should equal ¼ teaspoon.) Substitute 1 to 2 tablespoons orange rind in place of lemon rind and 1 tablespoon orange juice for lemon juice in icing.

LIME:
Follow directions above – except substitute ¼ teaspoon green liquid food coloring in place of yellow. Substitute 1 to 2 tablespoons lime rind in place of lemon rind and 1 tablespoon lime juice for lemon juice in icing.

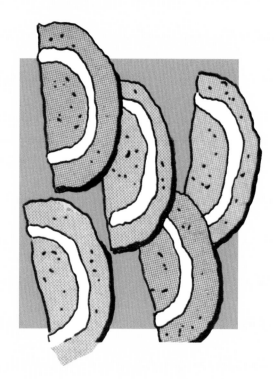

INGREDIENTS

1 cup soft butter

1 cup sifted confectioners' sugar

¼ teaspoon salt

¼ teaspoon yellow food coloring

1 to 2 tablespoons lemon rind

2½ cups flour

Yellow decorator's sugar

from *Candy Cookies*, circa 1950

INGREDIENTS

DOUGH ONE:

1 cup flour

½ cup sugar

5 tablespoons butter or margarine

Cream shortening and sugar and knead into flour.

DOUGH TWO:

1 cup flour

½ cup sugar

5 tablespoons butter or margarine

2 teaspoons instant coffee

DIRECTIONS

Preheat oven to 350°

Sieve flour and instant coffee together. Cream shortening and sugar and knead into flour.

Roll each dough onto waxed paper to equal sized oblong pieces, brush the plain one with milk. Press the coffee one on top, and roll up as for a jellyroll. Cut off pieces ⅛" thick.

Bake on a greased tray until pale golden.

Makes 16-18 wheels.

INGREDIENTS

PART 1:

¾ cup sifted flour

¼ teaspoon baking soda

¼ teaspoon salt

¼ cup butter or margarine

½ cup firmly packed brown sugar

½ egg well beaten

½ teaspoon vanilla

PART 2:

¾ cup sifted flour

¼ teaspoon baking soda

¼ teaspoon salt

¼ cup shortening

½ cup granulated sugar

½ egg well beaten

½ teaspoon vanilla

½ ounce unsweetened chocolate, melted

DIRECTIONS

Preheat oven to 375°

PART 1:

Mix and sift flour, baking soda and salt. Beat shortening until creamy. Add sugar gradually, continuing to beat until light. Add egg and vanilla and mix thoroughly. Gradually add flour mixture and mix well.

PART 2:

Mix as part 1, adding chocolate to the egg mixture.

Place each piece of dough on waxed paper. Roll out in a rectangle. Put chocolate dough on light dough, peel off papers. Roll. Wrap in wax paper and chill well.

Remove paper from dough, cut into ⅛" slices and place on greased baking sheets 1 ½" apart. Bake about 10 minutes.

Makes about 4 dozen.

from *Cooky Jar Favorites*, 1956

Shortbread Cookies

INGREDIENTS

1 cup margarine or butter

½ cup brown sugar

2 tablespoons granulated sugar

1 egg yolk

2 cups flour

½ teaspoon vanilla

1 tablespoon milk

DIRECTIONS

Preheat oven to 400°

Cream shortening and sugars together. Add egg yolk, vanilla and milk, and mix well. Blend in the flour. Mold the mixture by rounding teaspoonfuls into balls and place on baking sheets, and press flat with a fork that has been dipped in flour.

Bake 10 minutes. Remove immediately from baking sheets.

Makes about 5½ dozen.

from *Cookie-Craft*, circa 1940

INGREDIENTS

½ cup margarine or butter

⅔ cup brown sugar

1 egg yolk

1 cup flour

⅛ teaspoon cream of tartar

½ cup chopped pecans

Pecan halves

DIRECTIONS

Preheat oven to 325°

Cream shortening and sugar together. Add egg yolk and mix well. Add dry ingredients that have been sifted together. Add the chopped pecans. Mold the mixture by teaspoonfuls into balls and place on baking sheets.

Top each with a pecan half and bake 12-15 minutes. Remove immediately from baking sheets.

Makes about 1½ dozen.

from *Cookie-Craft*, circa 1940

INGREDIENTS

1 cup soft butter

¾ cup sifted confectioners' sugar

3 teaspoons vanilla

¾ teaspoon salt

½ cup uncooked (rolled) oats

2 cups flour

½ cup semi-sweet chocolate pieces

¼ cup milk

Finely chopped pecans or walnuts

Shredded coconut

Chocolate sprinkles

DIRECTIONS

Preheat oven to 325°

Mix well butter, sugar, and vanilla. Stir in salt, oats, and flour. With fingers, shape teaspoonfuls of dough into disks, balls, crescents, triangles and bars.

Bake on ungreased baking sheet 20-23 minutes or until golden around edges. Cool. Melt chocolate, add milk; blend until smooth. Dip cookies rounded side down in chocolate, then in nuts, coconut or sprinkles. Set on racks.

Makes about 4 dozen.

NOTE:
Watch baking time – easily over baked.

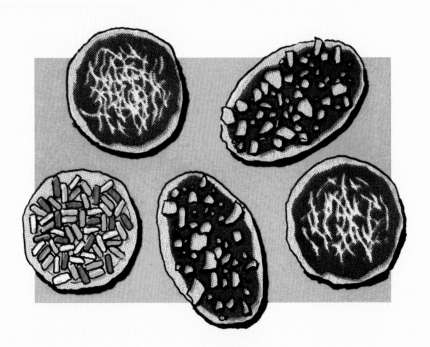

from *Candy Cookies*, circa 1950

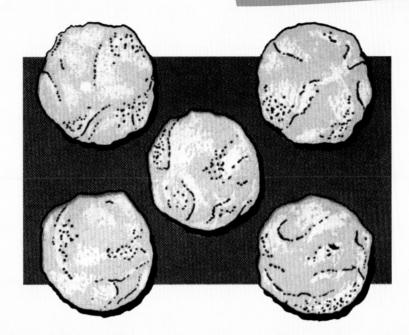

INGREDIENTS

1 cup butter or margarine

¾ cup sugar

1 egg

2½ cups flour

½ teaspoon baking powder

⅛ teaspoon salt

1 teaspoon vanilla

Whole filberts

60 sugar cubes (crushed) or coarse granulated sugar

DIRECTIONS

Preheat oven to 375°

Cream shortening and sugar. Add egg. Sift dry ingredients together. Blend with creamed mixture. Add vanilla. Roll into balls (using 1 level teaspoon dough per ball) and press a filbert in center. Shape so dough covers nut. Place on an ungreased baking sheet about 2″ apart.

Bake 12 to 15 minutes, until delicately browned. Cool. Dip entire top in glaze (recipe below), then in sugar.

Makes 7 to 8 dozen.

GLAZE:

Mix 2 cups sifted confectioners' sugar, 3 tablespoons water and 2 teaspoons vanilla.

from *Candy Cookies*, circa 1950

INGREDIENTS

½ cup soft butter or margarine

½ cup peanut butter

½ cup sugar

½ cup brown sugar (packed)

1 egg

1¼ cups flour

½ teaspoon baking powder

¾ teaspoon baking soda

¼ teaspoon salt

4 small plain chocolate bars, melted*

¾ cup salted peanuts, crushed

DIRECTIONS

Preheat oven to 375°

Mix shortening, peanut butter, sugars, egg thoroughly. Sift dry ingredients together; stir in. Chill about 1 hour. Put through cookie press, making 2½" length cookies. Use star shape plate. Bake on greased baking sheet about 2" apart.

Bake 8 to 10 minutes until lightly browned. When cool dip one end in melted chocolate and then in crushed peanuts.

Makes about 6 dozen cookies.

*Melt chocolate in a glass custard cup over hot water. Keep over hot water while dipping cookies.

from *Candy Cookies*, circa 1950

DIRECTIONS

Preheat oven to 400°

Cream shortening, add sugar, add eggs. Add flour mixed with cinnamon, cloves, baking soda and salt, mix well. Add rolled oats and raisins. If dough is not stiff enough to hold its shape add more rolled oats rather than flour to keep the consistency rough instead of smooth. Chill dough. Form into walnut-sized balls, roll in cinnamon-sugar and place on greased cookie sheets.

Bake 12 to 15 minutes.

INGREDIENTS

1 cup butter or margarine

1 cup sugar

2 eggs

cup milk

2 cups flour

2 cups rolled oats

1 cup raisins

1 teaspoon cinnamon

1 teaspoon cloves

¾ teaspoon baking soda

1 teaspoon salt

from *Cookbook* by Reddie Wilcolator

Nut Puffs

INGREDIENTS

1 cup butter or margarine

1 cup flour

½ cup confectioner's sugar

1 teaspoon vanilla

¾ cup chopped pecans

DIRECTIONS

Preheat oven to 375°

Blend flour and shortening with pastry blender, as for pie crust. Add vanilla and pecans and blend well. Dough will be some-what crumbly. Mold into 1″ balls. Place on an un-greased baking sheet 1″ apart.

Bake about 12-15 minutes puffs will be light in color. Roll in confectioners sugar immediately after baking.

Makes about 3 dozen cookies.

from *Praise for the Cook*, 1959

INGREDIENTS

½ cup butter or margarine

1 cup light brown sugar

½ cup peanut butter

1 egg

1½ cups sifted enriched flour

½ teaspoon salt

1 teaspoon baking soda

DIRECTIONS

Preheat oven to 375°

Blend shortening, brown sugar, peanut butter, salt and egg. Add mixed dry ingredients and mix thoroughly. Shape into 1″ balls. Place 2″ apart on un-greased baking sheets. Flatten by pressing crisscross with tines of fork.

Bake 10-12 minutes. Cool on baking sheets 2 to 3 minutes before removing. Makes about 4 dozen cookies.

from *Praise for the Cook,* 1959

Marzipan Cookies

INGREDIENTS

½ cup soft butter

¼ cup sugar

1¼ cups flour

Food coloring (see below)

⅛ teaspoon almond flavoring

DIRECTIONS

Preheat oven to 300°

Cream butter, sugar, food coloring of your choice (below) and flavoring. Stir in flour, mix thoroughly. Shape as directed; use 2 level teaspoonfuls of dough. Place on ungreased baking sheet; chill 30 minutes. Bake about 30 minutes (time will vary with size). Do not brown. Makes 2 to 2½ dozen.

YELLOW DOUGH: Add 2 to 3 drops yellow food coloring.

BANANAS: Roll dough into banana shape, curving and tapering ends. Flatten tops slightly. Paint on markings with mixture of 3 drops red, 2 drops yellow, 1 drop blue food coloring diluted with ½ teaspoon water.

from *Candy Cookies*, circa 1950

PEARS: Roll dough into a ball, then cone. Bend top slightly. Insert a piece of stick cinnamon for stem. For red blush dilute $\frac{1}{8}$ teaspoon red food coloring with 1 teaspoon water, paint cheeks.

APPLES: Roll dough into ball. Use small piece of cinnamon for stem and clove blossom in end. Add red blush as in pears.

PEACHES: Roll dough into ball. Make crease down one side with toothpick. Use clove in blossom end. Add red blush.

RED DOUGH: Add 4 to 5 drops red food coloring.

STRAWBERRIES: Roll dough into ball, then heart shape about ¾" high. For texture punch with blunt end of toothpick. Roll in red decorator's sugar. Use piece of green colored toothpick or green dough for stem.

CHERRIES: Roll 2 teaspoons dough into 3 small balls. Use piece of green colored toothpick for stem.

PLUMS: Follow directions for peaches. For blush, dilute $\frac{1}{8}$ teaspoon blue and 2 drops red food coloring with 1 teaspoon water.

ORANGE DOUGH: Add 3 drops red and 2 drops yellow food coloring.

ORANGES: Form into ball. Insert clove in blossom end. For texture punch with blunt end of toothpick.

APRICOTS: Follow directions for peaches. Use red blush.

CARROTS: Roll dough into 2" rolls; taper at end. Make stem as for strawberries.

GREEN DOUGH: Add 4 to 5 drops green food coloring.

GREEN APPLES: Follow directions for apples. Use red blush.

BEANS: Use ½ level teaspoon dough. Roll into 2" lengths (¼" in diameter). Curve slightly.

PEAS IN A POD: Use 1½ level teaspoonfuls of dough and form into flat 1½" circle. Divide level teaspoonfuls of dough into 3 or 4 equal parts; form peas. Place in center of circle, shape dough around peas. Pinch ends of pod together.

"Now Remember!"

INGREDIENTS

1 cup molasses

2 level teaspoons baking powder

3⅓ cups flour

2 teaspoons ginger

½ cup butter

1½ teaspoons salt

DIRECTIONS

Preheat oven to 350°

Boil the molasses two minutes and pour on the butter; cool. Sift together thoroughly the flour, baking powder, ginger and salt and add.

Chill, roll on a floured board as thin as possible. Cut into shapes and bake until lightly browned.

from *Reliable Recipes*, 1918

Sugar Cookies

INGREDIENTS

½ pound butter

1 cup sugar

2 eggs

1 tablespoon water

1 teaspoon vanilla extract (or substitute one teaspoon crushed caraway)

1 teaspoon baking powder

2½ cups flour

DIRECTIONS

Preheat oven to 400°

Cream butter and sugar thoroughly together with a wooden spoon. Beat eggs until very light, add to creamed mixture, beat well, add water and extract. To ½ cup flour add baking powder and sift into other ingredients, beat until light, and then add two cups flour and mix thoroughly. Turn out onto a floured baking board, knead lightly, roll out very thin and cut out with a cookie cutter.

Bake for 10 minutes.

Makes about 50 cookies.

from *Ryzon Baking Book*, 1917

Picture from
John Martin's Book, 1950

INGREDIENTS

1 egg

1 cup sugar

¼ cup melted butter or margarine

2 cups flour

½ teaspoon baking soda

1 teaspoon salt

1 cup buttermilk

2 cups graham flour

DIRECTIONS

Preheat oven to 350°

Beat egg until light and add sugar and short-ening. Mix and add flour sifted with baking soda and salt. Add buttermilk and graham flour. Mix well and add more flour if neces-sary. Chill. Roll out ⅛ inch thick and cut with a cookie cutter.

Bake on a floured cookie sheet until a delicate brown.

from *Good Things to Eat,* 1925

Magazine Illustration, 1927

INGREDIENTS

½ cup butter or margarine

1 cup sugar

2 eggs

2¾ cups flour

1 teaspoon baking powder

¼ teaspoon salt

¼ teaspoon nutmeg

Grated rind of 1 lemon

½ cup currants

Magazine Illustration, 1926

DIRECTIONS

Preheat oven to 400°

Cream the shortening and the sugar. Add the beaten eggs and milk. Mix and sift dry ingredients. Add lemon rind and stir in, adding currants with last of flour. Roll, cut in squares, brush over with milk.

Bake in a hot oven.

from *The Fairies Cookbook*, circa 1926

INGREDIENTS

½ cup butter or margarine

1 cup sugar

2 eggs

½ cup dark molasses

3½ cups flour

1 teaspoon salt

1 teaspoon baking powder

1 teaspoon soda

2 teaspoons ginger

⅓ cup boiling water

DIRECTIONS

Preheat oven to 350°

Blend shortening with sugar. Stir in eggs and molasses. Sift together flour, salt, baking powder, soda and ginger. Add alternately with water. When thoroughly mixed, roll to a thin sheet on lightly floured board. Cut half of dough with round cutter. Use doughnut cutter to cut remainder.

Bake on greased cookie sheet 8 to 10 minutes. When cool put together with creamy filling.

Makes 4 dozen.

CREAMY FILLING:
Blend 1 tablespoon butter or margarine with ½ cup sifted confectioners' sugar, ⅛ teaspoon salt and ⅛ teaspoon ginger. Beat in 1 tablespoon cream or milk. If necessary, add more confectioners' sugar to give a spreading consistency.

from *Recipes for Good Eating*, 1945

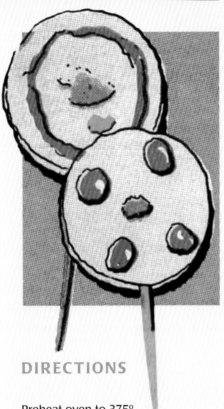

INGREDIENTS

1½ cups sifted confectioners' sugar

1 cup butter

1 egg

1 teaspoon vanilla

½ teaspoon almond flavoring

2½ cups flour

1 teaspoon baking soda

1 teaspoon cream of tartar

DIRECTIONS

Preheat oven to 375°

Mix sugar and butter. Add egg, flavorings; mix thoroughly. Sift dry ingredients; stir into butter mixture. Refrigerate 2 to 3 hours. Roll on lightly floured pastry cloth ³/₁₆″ thick. Cut into 1 ¼″ circles. Paint half the cookies with egg yolk paint (recipe below) Bake 6 to 8 minutes. To assemble spread easy creamy icing (recipe below) on flat side of baked cookie. Place a colored toothpick across the middle letting one end extend beyond edge of cookie. Place another cookie on top (flat sides together); press down slightly.

Makes 6 dozen.

EGG YOLK PAINT:
Blend I egg yolk, ¼ teaspoon water. Divide into 2 or 3 custard cups. Add food color as desired. Paint designs with small paintbrushes, using separate brush for each color. If paint thickens on standing, add a few drips of water.

EASY CREAMY ICING:
Blend 2 cups sifted confectioners' sugar, ½ teaspoon salt, 1 teaspoon vanilla or other flavoring add about 3 tablespoons cream.

from *Candy Cookies*, circa 1950

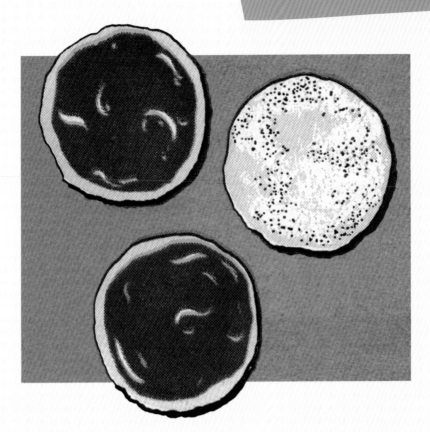

INGREDIENTS

1 cup soft butter

2 cups flour

½ cup sugar

1 cup finely chopped walnuts

DIRECTIONS

Preheat oven to 350°

Combine all ingredients and blend well. Roll dough on lightly floured, cloth covered board with rolling pin covered with stocking to ¼" (rather less than more). Cut with cookie cutter 1½" in diameter.

Bake 10 to 12 minutes on ungreased baking sheet. Cool. Cookies may be served plain, sprinkled with confectioners' sugar, frosted with bitter chocolate icing or stacked with raspberry jam.

Makes 8 dozen cookies.

from *Candy Cookies*, circa 1950

Berliner Kranser

INGREDIENTS

¾ cup butter or margarine

1 cup sugar

2 eggs

2 teaspoons grated orange peel

3¾ cups sifted flour

1 egg white

Red and green sugar

Red cinnamon candies

Citron cut in strips

Red candied cherries cut in quarters

DIRECTIONS

Preheat oven to 400°

Cream shortening, butter and sugar together; beat until well blended. Add eggs one at a time; beat well after each addition. Stir in orange peel. Add flour a little at a time; stir well until blended; chill until firm. On a lightly floured board, roll out dough ¼" thick and cut with a doughnut cutter. Place on ungreased cookie sheets. Brush tops with egg white. Decorate with red and green sugar and candies, citron and cherries.

Bake 10-12 minutes.

Makes about 6 dozen.

from *Foodarama Party Book,* 1959

INGREDIENTS

4 cups flour

½ teaspoon baking soda

¼ teaspoon salt

1 cup butter

2 cups sugar

3 eggs

1 teaspoon vanilla

Red and white confectioner's icing

Red cinnamon candies

Shredded coconut

Green sugar

DIRECTIONS

Preheat oven to 350°

Sift together flour, baking soda and salt. Cream butter, slowly add and beat in sugar and continue beating until well blended. Add eggs one at a time, beating well after each addition; blend in vanilla. Add sifted dry ingredients gradually; blend well. Cover bowl; chill dough for several hours, until firm enough to roll. Grease cookie sheets. On a lightly floured board, roll out chilled dough, ¼" thick. Cut with floured Santa Claus cookie cutter; place on cookie sheets.

Bake 8-10 minutes, or until cookies are golden. Run spatula under cookies to remove from sheets. Cool on wire racks. Decorate as shown with icing, candies, coconut and sugar.

Makes about 4 dozen.

from *Foodarama Party Book*, 1959

INGREDIENTS

½ cup butter or margarine

2 eggs, well beaten

1 tablespoon vanilla

2 teaspoons baking powder

Jelly

1 cup sugar

2 tablespoons cream

3½ cups sifted flour

½ teaspoon salt

DIRECTIONS

Preheat oven to 375°

In a mixing bowl, beat shortening until creamy. Add sugar gradually; continue to beat until light. Add eggs, cream and vanilla, beat well. Mix and sift flour, baking powder and salt. Stir into egg mixture, blend well. Shape into a ball, wrap in wax paper and chill one hour. Lightly sprinkle board with confectioner's sugar. Divide dough into 2 parts and roll out about ¼" thick. Cut half the dough with a 3" plain cutter. Dip cutter in confectioner's sugar each time. Place on lightly greased baking sheets 1½" apart. Cut remaining dough with a 3" doughnut cutter.

Bake about 8 minutes, until light brown. Cool on racks. Spread plain rounds with jelly, top with doughnut shaped cookies.

Makes about 1½ dozen.

from *Cooky Jar Favorites*, 1956

INGREDIENTS

1 cup butter

¾ cup light brown sugar

1 egg

3 tablespoons molasses

1 cup flour

1½ teaspoons baking soda

½ teaspoon ground cloves

½ teaspoon ginger

1 teaspoon cinnamon

DIRECTIONS

Preheat oven to 375°

Cream butter and add sugar, egg and molasses. Beat well. Mix dry ingredients together and add to butter/sugar mixture. Chill dough. Roll ¼" thick on floured board. Cut into desired shapes with floured cookie cutters. Place on greased baking sheets.

Bake 8-10 minutes or until browned.

Makes about 3-4 dozen cookies.

from *Praise for the Cook*, 1959

TIPS ON STORING COOKIES

1. Store crisp cookies in a cookie jar or container with a tight fitting cover.

2. Store soft cookies in a cookie jar or container with a loose fitting cover.

3. Put a section of apple or a slice of bread in the container to help keep soft cookies fresh. Change apple or bread as it dries out.

4. If cookies are fragile, store in single layers, with a sheet of waxed paper between layers.

PUT COOKIES ON THE ROAD:

They travel well. They make personal, loving gifts for all ages. Use a heavy box, line with wax paper and place a layer of soft filler on the bottom. Wrap flat cookies back to back in pairs, in wax paper. Wrap all others separately. Fit wrapped in cookies snugly in layers. Use filler between layers, over top of last layer and to plug any gaps. There should be enough packing to keep cookies from rattling.

FREEZING:

The unbaked dough can be frozen in rolls or containers, ready to be used. Baked cookies, wrapped in moisture-proof, crush-proof packages will keep for a long time; and they defrost in a matter of minutes.

Picture from *Good Cooking Made Easy: Spry the Flavor Saver*, 1942

ADDITIONAL PICTURE CREDITS

Cover:	George R. Showalter, c. 1946.
Front Endpaper:	Corinne Dillon. from *Who Will Play With Me?* 1951.
Back Endpapers, Pages 4-5:	Corinne Pauli Waterall. from *At Play - Easy Growth in Reading* 1940.
Frontispiece:	Mildred Lyon Hetherington. from *Girls and Boys at School*, 1956.
Title Page:	Beth Henninger Krush. Magazine cover, 1958.
Copyright Page:	from pamphlet "Do-it-together" Butter Cookies
Table of contents:	George Tobin. Magazine cover.
Back Cover:	Unknown. Magazine illustration.

Picture from *Story Animals and Other Stories*, 1942